How We Did It
A Guide for Juvenile and Emerging Adult Offenders Ready for Positive Reform

Leah B. Mazzola, PhD

DEDICATION

To every young person with a history of offending who has ever doubted their potential - no past must define your future. Positive reform is within your grasp, but you must reach for it and work for it. It can be done. When you're ready, I hope this guide helps.

To my brother, Ralph Jr., and cousin, Thomas O., (who were murdered by peers at 16 before they could commit to the desistance and positive change that may have saved their lives) - You are my highest inspiration for this work; to shine the light for other young people as they transform their lives before it's too late. Your legacy lives on through everyone this work helps.

Table of Contents

Preface

This is intended to serve as a simplified quick reference guide to positive reform for criminal or juvenile offenders ready to do that work. It was developed as an extension of the study I conducted for my doctoral dissertation in forensic psychology, *A Phenomenological Inquiry into Identity Change on the Path to Long-term Criminal Desistance*. This booklet includes a brief overview of desistance research (Part I), a summary of the research-based desistance process (Part II), and reflection questions relevant to a successful desistance process to support young people as they begin to think through and prepare for positive reform. Please refer to the reference list for a link to the published study for the extended literature review and other supporting evidence.

For youth and emerging adults who can use individual support through this process, I provide desistance and positive reform coaching in-person for those local to the Dallas, TX metroplex and virtually via online meetings, internationally. For professionals who support youth and emerging adults through this process, I provide desistance and positive reform coach training internationally through Youth Coaching Institute, LLC. Learn more about coaching or training at youthcoachinginstitute.com.
E-mail: leah@youthcoachinginstitute.com.

Part 1: Desistance Research

"I just came to a place where I knew I didn't want to live like this anymore. I wanted to do something more with myself. I wanted a better life than I had growing up."
– Desistor

"I had to fall off the map. I went from getting high with friends every day for five years straight to staying clean, gettin' an office job, and workin' every day. I had to stay away from anyone and anything that could pull me back, and just keep pushin' forward."
- Desistor

First off, this topic matters because too many people don't think they can change harmful behaviors for good. I was lucky enough to survive and maintain my freedom long enough to do better, be better, and know better. I lived a lifestyle of delinquency and heavy, hard drug abuse from the ages of 12-17. At 17, I decided to do better with my life. I chose to stop my harmful behaviors and replace them with working to build a life I could be proud of. Through that work, I made it out to achieve success in ways I never would've dreamed of back then.

Sadly, I have close loved ones who lost their lives to early death, and those who lost their freedom and opportunities to long-term sentences or addictions that keep them down. The sobering reality of those outcomes fuels my passion for this work. I write this for those who don't believe positive, long-term change is possible, or that they're worth the time and effort. It is and you are. Plenty have succeeded before you. Keep reading to find out how we made it happen and get to work while there's still time. You and your life are too valuable to waste. You have so much good to offer this world. You just need to figure out what that is and use it well.

Now, please bear with me for a quick overview of the technical stuff to be sure you understand the terms that I'll use through this booklet. It's important that I introduce you to the terms - criminal desistance, desistance, and desistors, because those are the terms you can use to search for more helpful science on this topic.

To desist is to stop doing something. Criminal desistance is a person's transition from committing crimes (offending) to no longer committing crimes (non-offending). For juveniles, usually ages 10-18, that would be a transition from committing delinquent acts (offending) to not committing delinquent acts (non-offending). For reader ease, the term desistance will be used throughout this book when referring to desistance from crime. The term desistor will be used to describe a person working through that change – offender to non-offender.

Desistance is a process of behavior change that happens over time. The same way a person adapts to any other lifestyle. Offenders may adapt to offending as their normal lifestyle. Desistors then, must adapt to or re-adapt to no longer offending and find less harmful ways to meet their needs or reach their goals. That is positive reform.

Desistance researchers have been investigating this experience for over 30 years directly from those who experienced it. They investigate why ex-offenders stopped offending to understand *What went right?* for them. Ideally, offenders or people in the community who support their positive reform in some way would then, use that information as a guide to success. Makes sense, right? We're usually more willing to hear from people who've shared our struggles and found a way to succeed, regardless. That knowledge is what this booklet is here to share with you.

My desistance expertise comes from three primary sources 1) personal experience as a long-term desistor 2) as a desistance researcher who contributed to this knowledge-base through my doctoral dissertation, and 3) as a mentor and coach who supports desistors' positive reform. The knowledge and activities shared in this booklet will come from the combination of first-hand experience, in-depth research, and practice.

Part 2: How We Did It

"...at 16, I really made a decision that I'm gonna do whatever I have to, to get out of this crap." –
Desistor

"I always knew I was going to make my life better no matter what." – Desistor

When you're ready to consider doing better, here's a summary of what decades of research on successful desistors has found. Know, those desistors cared enough to share what worked for them, so you'd have a map to the other side too. As a desistor, I can confirm the list you'll read through next fit my experience on every point. Remember, desistance is a step-by-step process. Just consider one at a time. Then, move onto the next chapter where you'll have a chance to reflect on these things in your own life more deeply and prepare for your restart:

- o They came to a point where they were no longer okay with who they were as an offender, they recognized a potential future self they didn't want to be, and envisioned a future self they would rather be[1]

- o They wanted to change[2]

- o They had a sense of ownership to choose and do what they needed to do to make the change[3] o They made the decision to change[4]

o They had clear future goals, and came up with plans, and action steps to achieve those goals[5]

o They were confident they could do what needed to be done to achieve those goals[6]

o They actively self-regulated while pursuing their goals – That included, no longer doing things that could interfere with their goals and doing more of what could help them achieve their goals[7]

o They distanced themselves from situations, people, and places that would interfere with their goals and spent more time with people, places, and situations that would support their goals (e.g., non-offenders, education, and employment)[8] [9]

o They developed new identities associated with new roles they were pursuing (e.g., student, working professional, mentor)[10]

o And eventually achieved a place of no longer identifying with the criminal or delinquent self[11]

To contribute to this research, I focused my study on understanding the identity change factor of desistance – those last two bullets on the list. I interviewed a group of long-term desistors, people who were 10 or more years on the other side of positive change, to understand what led to the successful identity change from offender to non-offender, and what behaviors supported that change. It helped me better understand how the factors on the list above worked together to support successful outcomes. Here's a visual of the whole process followed by descriptions and examples of each one:

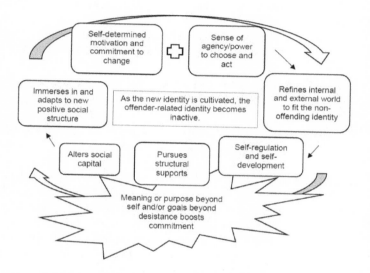

The first things they needed were:

✓ A self-determined commitment to become the non-offending self who they wanted to be

   Example: *I want to be better and do better. I will be better and do better. I will build a good life for myself.*

✓ A sense of ownership to choose and do what they needed to do to become the non-offender

Example: *I got this. No matter what. I got this.*

The behaviors were – The desistor:
1. began refining self to fit the non-offender they wanted to be by prioritizing self-control and self-development. This involved

   - using existing strengths, traits, and skills helpful to the non-offender, and

   - learning and developing new skills helpful to the non-offender

   - while working to stop using those that would hold them back.

Example: *I work hard when I need to and I'm good with people. I can figure out how to do things if it really matters. I just need to work on my patience and be willing to learn new things, even if it's hard and frustrating. My anger gets me in trouble. I need to learn to breathe and walk it off instead of blowing up on people.*

2. identified and pursued accessible structural supports helpful to non-offending (most often - school, work, and/or family, friends, or groups who are non-offenders)

Example: *I went back for my GED and now I'm in trade school. I got a job that pays enough to take care of what I need to. I only spend time with the people I know aren't making trouble.*

3. altered social capital toward people who fit

the non-offender life and away from people who did not fit the non-offender life

Example: *I stay away from anyone I know isn't staying out of trouble themselves. I can't have people dragging me down or trying to make me feel bad for doing something better with my life. I don't have time for that anymore. I only have time for people who support my rise.*

4. and remained actively engaged in chosen helpful environments using them to guide behavior change to develop the non-offender identity.

Example: *I listen, watch, and learn more than I ever did before. I pay attention to what successful people are doing and learn from them. I always find new ways to improve myself to be more likely to succeed.*

5. Through these efforts, the non-offender identity grows and the offender identity becomes inactive.

Example: *One day I realized I'm not even that person anymore. There's an old me and a new me. People who know me now wouldn't even believe how I used to live.*

6. The ongoing commitment to the non-offender identity is enhanced as desistors identify and use purpose outside of self on the other side of desistance as a booster fuel to succeed.

Example: *People are depending on me. I have*

responsibilities. I feel like I have something to offer, something to contribute now. I want to prove people can change. Stereotypes can be broken. Don't judge a book by its cover. I will be successful in life. I will build the life I want the right way. I will show other kids who grew up like I did that they can make a better life for themselves. They don't have to settle for what they know. They can create something better.

The next chapter offers some question and answer prompts to help you figure out if you're ready for positive change. Take your time going through it and be real about it.

Part 3: Are You Ready?

"I just said, I need to take control of this. And, that's where it started to happen." – Desistor

"I had an extreme desire to succeed...I took all my powers for evil and I used them for good. I changed the polarity of my life..." – Desistor

"Back then, I thought I was a badass because I was hard. I was a straight hood rat. You couldn't touch me. I was doing stupid shit, but I thought I was pretty awesome. Now, I have life to be proud of. I'm in college. I'm working full-time and earning my way into leadership positions, because I work hard and focus on doing what I have to do. That same hard head that kept me alive in the hood is what keeps me focused and untouchable at work." – Desistor

The following questions are intended to help you begin to reflect on your life as it is now, what it could be in the future, and what you can do between now and then to create a future you want. You can consider your answers to these questions privately, with a pen and paper, or out loud with a trusted, non-judgmental counselor, coach, mentor, loved one, or other supportive adult. It will be important that you think about each question deeply and take your time opening your mind to consider what's possible. You may not be able to get through all of these questions and answers in one sitting. It may be best to work through a handful at a time over several weeks. Just be sure you get through them all, because they do all matter to setting you up for success.

Are you happy with who you are at this point in your life and/or where you are at this point in your life? Why or why not?

What do you believe could happen to you or your loved ones if you continue offending? How do you imagine your future self in 10 years on this track?

Can you imagine a future self that you would rather be, and/or a future life you would rather have?

Why would it matter to achieve the future life you'd rather have?

Do you want to change the problem behavior? Why or why not?

Do you believe you can change the problem behavior? Why or why not?

Where and when do your choice points come up? Think of the moments when you have the power to choose to do better.

Will you change the problem behavior? Why or why not?

If you are committed to doing better, what future will you build for yourself on the other side? What are your goals? Be specific.

1.

2.

3.

What do you need to do to achieve your goals? Break your big goals down into smaller process goals. Like beating the game one strategic move at a time.

Which of your natural strengths and skills will you use to achieve your goals?

How confident are you that you can do what you need to do to achieve your goals?
Rate your confidence on a scale from 0 to 10 with 0 being not confident at all and 10 being very confident.

If you're not as confident as you would like to be, what do you believe you need to be more confident?

What education or job goals will be important to your success? Why?

How do you plan to use your education or job to support you as you build the life you want to live?

Who could you spend more time with as you work to achieve your goals? Why will that be important?

Who will you need to spend less time with as you work to achieve your goals? Why will that be important?

What behaviors will you need to do less or stop to achieve your goals? Why will that be important?

What behaviors will you need to start or do more to achieve your goals? Why will that be important?

What positive, supportive resources can you leverage through the process? Think of positive people, places, books, videos, etc.

Are you ready to start working toward your goals? If so, what's your first step? How will you take it? When will you begin?

What:

How:

When:

What obstacles are most likely to get in your way? How will you handle them?

Create your motto to inspire you when it gets tough. Mine was and still is: *No past must define your future.* **What's yours?**

In closing, know you can make positive changes. Trust yourself and those who love and support you the most. Trust the changes will come one choice at a time - one action step at a time. Reach out for the helpful support you need. If you have compassionate, non-judgmental family members or friends, connect with them for support. If you don't, there are so many caring professionals in the community who commit their lives to this work — mentors, coaches, therapists, social workers, teachers, leaders, and others. Find them. Connect with them. Pay attention and learn from them. Fight to overcome and thrive. Then, reach back and help someone else do the same.

About the Author

Leah B. Mazzola, PhD

My passion for coaching young people through positive reform is two-fold. First, personal experience with quantum change in life, relationships, and career means I know a single choice today to change your tomorrows is a powerful place to be. I grew up at-risk and transitioned to high-risk in early adolescence. I grew up one of seven children in a low-income, dysfunctional and abusive household, lost a 16-year-old brother and cousin to homicide by peers over drugs, a 16-year-old brother to a 25-year prison sentence, and a 16-year-old cousin to suicide. I spent my teens involved in delinquency, drug abuse, and other harmful behaviors that I now dedicate my life to helping other young people avoid or transition away from. I came to my "aha" moment at 17, made drastic changes, and made it out to achieve personal, academic, and professional success thought beyond my reach as a teen. I know, first-hand, that dramatic change is not only possible but immediately available to anyone committed to it. My life's purpose is to help other young people find success through positive, long-term change and achieve the potential they often don't realize they have.

Second, over a decade of formal study and research into delinquency and positive reform means I understand the science behind the process. Personal, professional, and social development are the keys to create the outcomes we seek. Each begins with self-exploration and self-mastery; and grow with focused work. Unfortunately, there's no way around the work part. That's where coaching comes in. I discovered the power of coaching through my doctoral studies as I investigated why some high-risk youth overcome the barriers to success while others do not. This research led me to coaching as a positive and empowering social support to enhance desistors' chances of success.

Coaching is a person-centered, strength-based, collaborative support service to help functional clients achieve meaningful goals. Coaching provides the structural support clients need to maximize their personal and professional potential. Coaching emphasizes autonomy, choice, and trust. Clients come to coaching with an interest in self-improvement or measurable progress. Through coaching, clients find insight and direction to identify practical means to reach their goals. The coach guides and supports the client's planned, intentional, and purposeful action toward achievement. Coaching clients are ready and willing to do the work inherent in the coaching process. They are committed to maximizing their internal and external resources to achieve the outcomes they seek.

My work is grounded in contextual behavioral science and choice theory. My coaching approach is pragmatic and evidence-based. To summarize those ideas, our thoughts, emotions, and behaviors are instruments that serve a purpose and contribute to our outcomes. We can create positive outcomes from the inside out through self-insight, practical strategies, and consistent, meaningful, targeted action. I coach to promote clients' rationality, agency, and attention to knowledge and skills development relevant to their goals. Feel free to reach out to me by E-mail at leah@youthcoachinginstitute.com, if you can use this type of support.

Lastly, here's a snapshot of myself just prior to my commitment to change beside the future self I evolved into through my desistance and positive reform journey:

Delinquent (16-years-old) to Doctor (34-years-old)

---

[1] Ronet Bachman et al. "Desistance for a Long-Term Drug-Involved Sample of Adult Offenders: The Importance of Identity Transformation." *Criminal Justice and Behavior* 43, no. 2 (February 2016): 164–86.

Sinéad Gormally. "'I've Been There, Done That...': A Study of Youth Gang Desistance." *Youth Justice* 15, no. 2 (August 2015): 148–65.

Michael Hallett and J. Stephen McCoy. "Religiously Motivated Desistance: An Exploratory Study." *International Journal of Offender Therapy and Comparative Criminology* 59, no. 8 (July 2015)

Gilly Sharpe. "Precarious Identities: 'Young' Motherhood,

Desistance and Stigma." *Criminology & Criminal Justice* 15, no. 4 (September 2015): 407–22.

[2] Gormally. 'I've Been There, Done That...,'148–65.

Hallett and McCoy. "Religiously Motivated Desistance

Thomas Søgaard, Birgitte Kolind, and Ross Deuchar. "Desistance and the Micro-Narrative Construction of Reformed Masculinities in a Danish Rehabilitation Centre." *Criminology & Criminal Justice* 16, no. 1 (February 2016): 99–118.

[3] Isabelle Dufour, Renée Brassard, and Joane Martel. "An Integrative Approach to Apprehend Desistance." *International Journal of Offender Therapy and Comparative Criminology* 59, no. 5 (May 2015): 480–501.

Elanie Rodermond, Candace Kruttschnitt, Anne-Marie Slotboom, and Catrien Bijleveld. "Female Desistance: A Review of the Literature." *European Journal of Criminology* 1-26.

Sharpe. "Precarious Identities," 407–22.

[4] Bachman et al. "Desistance for a Long-Term Drug-Involved Sample of Adult Offenders," 164–86.

Nienke Liebregts, Peggy van der Pol, Ron de Graaf, Margriet van Laar, Wim van den Brink & Dirk J. Korf. "Persistence and Desistance in Heavy Cannabis Use: The Role of Identity, Agency, and Life Events." Journal of Youth Studies, 18, 5 (2015): 617-633

Diane Terry and Laura Abrams. "Dangers, Diversions, and Decisions: The Process of Criminal Desistance Among Formerly Incarcerated Young Men." *International Journal of Offender Therapy and Comparative Criminology* 61, no. 7 (May 2017): 727–50.

[5] Bachman et al. "Desistance for a Long-Term Drug-Involved Sample of Adult Offenders," 164–86.

Liebregts et al. "Persistence and Desistance in Heavy Cannabis Use." 617-633.

Terry and Abrams. "Dangers, Diversions, and Decisions." 727–50.

[6] Liebregts et al. "Persistence and Desistance in Heavy Cannabis Use." 617-633.

Rodermond, Kruttschnitt, Slotboom, and Bijleveld. "Female Desistance." 1-26.

Søgaard, Kolind, and Deuchar. "Desistance and the Micro-Narrative Construction of Reformed Masculinities." 99–118.

Terry and Abrams. "Dangers, Diversions, and Decisions." 727–50.

[7] Bachman et al. "Desistance for a Long-Term Drug-Involved Sample of Adult Offenders," 164–86.

Liebregts et al. "Persistence and Desistance in Heavy Cannabis Use." 617-633.

Valli Rajah, Ronald Kramer, and Hung-En Sung. "Changing Narrative Accounts: How Young Men Tell Different Stories When Arrested, Enduring Jail Time and Navigating Community Reentry." Punishment & Society 16, no. 3 (July 2014): 285–304.

Søgaard, Kolind, and Deuchar. "Desistance and the Micro-Narrative Construction of Reformed Masculinities." 99–118.

Terry and Abrams. "Dangers, Diversions, and Decisions." 727–50.

[8] Dufour, Brassard, and Martel. "An Integrative Approach to Apprehend Desistance." 480–501.

Rodermond, Kruttschnitt, Slotboom, and Bijleveld. "Female Desistance." 1-26.

Sharpe. "Precarious Identities," 407–22.

[9] Hallett and McCoy. "Religiously Motivated Desistance

Gormally. 'I've Been There, Done That…,'148–65.

Liebregts et al. "Persistence and Desistance in Heavy Cannabis Use." 617-633.

[10] Sharpe. "Precarious Identities," 407–22.

Bachman et al. "Desistance for a Long-Term Drug-Involved Sample of Adult Offenders," 164–86.

[11] Bachman et al. "Desistance for a Long-Term Drug-Involved Sample of Adult Offenders," 164–86.

Liebregts et al. "Persistence and Desistance in Heavy Cannabis Use." 617-633.

Terry and Abrams. "Dangers, Diversions, and Decisions." 727–50.

References

Ronet Bachman, Erin Kerrison, Raymond Paternoster, Daniel O'Connell, and Lionel Smith. "Desistance for a Long-Term Drug-Involved Sample of Adult Offenders: The Importance of Identity Transformation." Criminal Justice and Behavior 43, no. 2 (February 2016): 164–86. doi:10.1177/0093854815604012.

Isabelle Dufour, Renée Brassard, and Joane Martel. "An Integrative Approach to Apprehend Desistance." International Journal of Offender Therapy and Comparative Criminology 59, no. 5 (May 2015): 480–501. doi:10.1177/0306624X13509781.

Sinéad Gormally. "'I've Been There, Done That…': A Study of Youth Gang Desistance." Youth Justice 15, no. 2 (August 2015): 148–65. doi:10.1177/1473225414549679.

Michael Hallett and J. Stephen McCoy. "Religiously

    Motivated Desistance: An Exploratory Study."

    International Journal of Offender Therapy and

    Comparative Criminology 59, no. 8 (July 2015):

    855–72. doi:10.1177/0306624X14522112.

Nienke Liebregts, Peggy van der Pol, Ron de Graaf,

    Margriet van Laar, Wim van den Brink & Dirk J.

    Korf (2015) Persistence and desistance in heavy

    cannabis use: the role of identity, agency, and life

    events, Journal of Youth Studies, 18:5, 617-633

Leah Mazzola. "A Phenomenological Inquiry into Identity

    Change on the Path to Long-term Criminal

    Desistance." ScholarWorks. (2016) Retrieved from

    https://scholarworks.waldenu.edu

Valli Rajah, Ronald Kramer, and Hung-En Sung.

    "Changing Narrative Accounts: How Young Men

    Tell Different Stories When Arrested, Enduring Jail

    Time and Navigating Community Reentry."

    Punishment & Society 16, no. 3 (July 2014): 285–

    304. doi:10.1177/1462474514527148.

Elanie Rodermond, Candace Kruttschnitt, Anne-Marie
    Slotboom, and Catrien Bijleveld. "Female
    Desistance: A Review of the Literature." *European
    Journal of Criminology.* (2015) 1-26.
    doi:10.1177/1477370815597251

Gilly Sharpe. "Precarious Identities: 'Young' Motherhood,
    Desistance and Stigma." Criminology & Criminal
    Justice 15, no. 4 (September 2015): 407–22.
    doi:10.1177/1748895815572163.

Thomas Søgaard, Birgitte Kolind, and Ross Deuchar.
    "Desistance and the Micro-Narrative Construction
    of Reformed Masculinities in a Danish
    Rehabilitation Centre." Criminology & Criminal
    Justice 16, no. 1 (February 2016): 99–118.
    doi:10.1177/1748895815599582.

Diane Terry and Laura Abrams. "Dangers, Diversions,
    and Decisions: The Process of Criminal
    Desistance Among Formerly Incarcerated Young
    Men." International Journal of Offender Therapy

and Comparative Criminology 61, no. 7 (May

2017): 727–50. doi:10.1177/0306624X15602704.